MW01119535

Praise for *Chasing the Wind*

Robert White has captured the great questions of life and brought us back to the foundation that helps us make sense of these questions. Men need to see the merging of biblical truth with answers to real life questions, and this look at the book of Ecclesiastes accomplishes that.

Kirk Giles, President
Promise Keepers Canada

In any popularity poll, the biblical book of Ecclesiastes would not rank very highly. It has only 11 chapters, which the *Reader's Digest Family Guide to the Bible* describes as "deeply pessimistic." Even the book's name puts people off—it reeks of stuffy churchiness.

Any cursory skimming of the book suggests that its primary theme is the futility and meaninglessness of life.

So when journalist Robert White encountered a series of life problems—with his physical body, his employment, his Christian faith—that made him wonder if his own efforts were also as meaningless as chasing the wind, he turned to Ecclesiastes. He found there, beneath the pessimism, a profound depth of insight, of wisdom, and even wit.

In this book, *Chasing the Wind*, White weaves together themes from the ancient writer—whoever he was; the message matters more than the authorship—with illustrations from his own life, contemporary contexts, and the Christian gospels. It's more than Bible study; it's an exploration of life, of faith, of humanity.

And to help readers focus on those issues, White includes with each chapter some suggested questions for discussion or internal reflection.

Reading Ecclesiastes in tandem with Robert White's *Chasing the Wind* will, I have no doubt, offer readers a multitude of valuable insights.

James Taylor

Author of *An Everyday God* and 15 other books on contemporary religious practices

Co-founder of Wood Lake Books publishing house

Founding editor of *PMC: Practice of Ministry in Canada*; former managing editor, *The United Church Observer* (United Church of Canada)

As someone who loves the book of Ecclesiastes and teaches from it often, Robert's book is an excellent summary of the content of this ancient book of wisdom. As a long time student of this book I believe he gets it right when it comes to what this ancient manuscript is really all about. Robert clearly explains the ancient wisdom of this book in a way that is easy to understand as a person in the twenty first century. He uses excellent illustrations from his own life journey and many cultural illustrations to highlight the applicable aspects of the book of Ecclesiastes to real life today. He doesn't only examine the pessimistic nature of this writing but highlights the hope that this ancient wisdom provides. The way he divides and subdivides the book, he clearly articulates the major themes of the book. The discussion questions at the end of each chapter provide a great framework for a personal devotional study or as a study for a small group. I am thankful to Robert for some of the new insights he gave me as I read and pondered all over again one of my favourite Bible books. He truly does provide meaningful answers to the real world from this ancient book of wisdom.

DAVID RALPH, LEAD PASTOR
Lakeside Church in Guelph

Chasing the Wind is a contemporary take on the age-old problem of discovering lasting meaning in the ordinary affairs of life.

The things that seem to matter most are apt to melt away like mirages as soon as we get close. All the wealth, wisdom and accomplishment imaginable can turn to exhaust fumes in our minds. The total sum of human experience is as futile as chasing the wind unless—and this is the last word—the questing individual actually focuses full attention on God and makes keeping his commandments the key to the day-to-day conduct of his or her life. Wealth that satisfies, wisdom that endures and accomplishments that matter are by-products of a God-centred life. Aim for them, and risk missing life. Set your sights on God to discover purpose and meaning.

Robert White's new book is a series of short, practical reflections on life based on the book of Ecclesiastes. *Chasing the Wind* can be read at a single sitting or mulled over for weeks in a group study. It discusses the normal passages of life, acknowledging the inevitable twist and turns and ups and downs. It ends on a note of hope. Mere life on earth can never be fully satisfying to people, who were created with eternity in our hearts.

DOUG KOOP, EDITORIAL DIRECTOR
Christian Week

Chasing the Wind is an incredible look at what one of the Bible's most poetic books has to say about being alive today. Practical, relevant, easy to read and beautifully crafted—the times I spent pondering Robert White's insights were filled with laughter, tears, and the reminder to live each day in the light of God's eternal wisdom.

MAGS STOREY
Journalist and award-winning
author of *If Only You Knew*

Finding Meaningful Answers from Ancient Wisdom

Robert White

CHASING THE WIND: FINDING MEANINGFUL ANSWERS FROM ANCIENT WISDOM

ISBN: 978–1–77069–144–5

Printed in Canada.

Word Alive Press
131 Cordite Road, Winnipeg, MB R3W 1S1

Library and Archives Canada Cataloguing in Publication

White, Robert, 1960-

Chasing the wind : finding meaningful answers from ancient wisdom / Robert White.

ISBN 978-1-77069-144-5

1. Bible. O.T. Ecclesiastes--Commentaries. 2. Wisdom--Religious aspects--Christianity. I. Title.

BS1475.53.W55 2010 223'.807 C2010-907220-0

Author photo by: Anderson-Coats Photography

To my wife, Pam, and my children, Tim and Kathleen, who put up with my endless absences, distractions, and preoccupations as I honed the craft of writing and finished this book.

ACKNOWLEDGMENTS

The act of writing is typically a solo endeavour that takes place when a writer sits in front of a blank screen and sweats drops of blood until words pour onto the screen. The act of authoring a book is a community effort in which the writer's life experience—including the lives of people he's met and touched—is poured forth into what he or she hopes will have an effect on others.

Chasing the Wind is no different. While the words (and errors) are mine and mine alone, the book is the work of a community. And to that community I owe an unpayable debt of gratitude:

Those who have ever read a newspaper column, listened to a sermon, or sat in a Bible study which eventually formed the basis of this book.

Marg Buchanan, Right Reverend Peter Moore, Reverend Royal Hamel, Karen Stiller, and Krysia Lear—all of whom read early drafts of this book and contributed to its eventual development.

My colleagues at *ChristianWeek*, all the editors I've ever written for, my friends in The Word Guild (especially Kathleen Gibson), and anyone who ever encouraged me to keep writing.

Evan Braun, Caroline Schmidt, and the rest of the Word Alive Press staff who have worked hard to make this dream a reality.

Pam, my wife, who has read every word of this book in its various incarnations and has provided invaluable feedback and advice. Tim and Kathleen who, by virtue of being my children, find themselves in—but hopefully not embarrassed by—the pages of this book.

TABLE OF CONTENTS

SAYS THE TEACHER

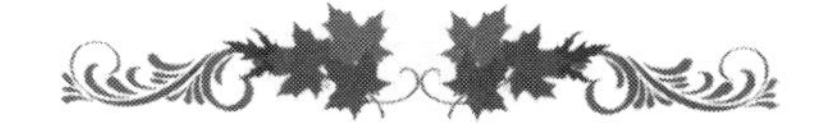

Then I observed that most people are motivated to success because they envy their neighbors. But this, too, is meaningless—like chasing the wind.
(Ecclesiastes 4:4, NLT)

All we are is dust in the wind (Kansas)

I began studying Ecclesiastes scant months before two critical events—the birth of my first child, a son, and the death of my father. Journaling about these events, I wrote:

> Reading the Beacon Commentary and the intro to Ecclesiastes in the

> Good News Bible, I realize at this moment how this book will speak to me. I've been feeling frustrated about my job, the ministry, the church, and my future. I've often found myself crying out to God about the futility of my life and the direction it's taking.
>
> Perhaps as I read Ecclesiastes I can find some of the answers to what I feel is a seemingly meaningless, useless, and empty life for me at the moment. I can't say all the questions have been answered, but at least I know there was one person who understood the meaninglessness of life.

What I found in Ecclesiastes was, in the words of the Reader's Digest Family Guide to the Bible, a "deeply pessimistic"[1] book. Ecclesiastes speaks of

---

1 Editors of Readers Digest. *Reader's Digest Family Guide to the Bible: A Concordance and Reference Companion to the King James Version* (Pleasantville, NY: Readers Digest, 1984) p. 22.

having, wanting, and the futility of both. Listing the accomplishments of a king of Israel in the first three chapters, the writer concludes, "*Then I observed that most people are motivated to success because they envy their neighbors. But this, too, is meaningless—like chasing the wind*" (Ecclesiastes 4:4, NLT).

One of the best modern images of this ancient wisdom comes from an episode of one of my favourite television shows: *Star Trek*. In the original series classic episode "Amok Time," Spock goes home to the planet Vulcan to rid himself of the "blood fever," caused by the Vulcan mating cycle. The episode's climax featured a hand–to–hand battle to the death between Spock and his best friend and commanding officer, James T. Kirk. When the fight was over, Kirk seemingly lay dead aboard the orbiting *U.S.S Enterprise*.

With the blood fever gone, Spock asked his fiancée T'pring why she had chosen the challenge and why she wanted Kirk as her champion. T'pring explained that she knew Spock loved his career more than her and that while he was flying around space in the *Enterprise*, she'd fallen in love with another man, Stonn. She knew that no matter who won—Kirk or Spock—she'd end up with her new love.

Spock praised T'pring's flawless logic and broke off the engagement. Then, turning to Stonn, Spock said, "You may find that *having* is not, after all, so satisfying a thing as *wanting*."

First Impressions

The more I delved into Ecclesiastes, the more I saw the truth in Spock's words—especially since I needed to correct my first impressions of it. As a teen I heard a few now long–forgotten sermons based on its opening words as found in the King James Version: *"vanity of vanities"* (Ecclesiastes 1:2).

My young mind equated vanity with the Farah Fawcett poster which became an icon of the 70s. The buxom beauty in the red swimsuit with windswept, layered blond hair graced many a teenage boy's bedroom after its 1976 release. While many high school girls tried to replicate Fawcett's locks, vanity wasn't something I worried much about as a short, dumpy, prepubescent teenager. For me, "vanity" was a word in the dictionary that fell between "vanitory" and "vanquish."

My second introduction to Ecclesiastes came from the 60s' folk rock group The Byrds, who scored a number one hit with the Pete Seeger–written "Turn, Turn, Turn (To Everything a Season)." After this opening chorus:

> To everything turn, turn, turn
>
> There is a season turn, turn, turn
>
> And a time for every purpose under heaven.[2]

Seeger quotes Ecclesiastes 3:1–8. While I always liked the lilting ditty, singing it at church campfires and youth groups, it wasn't until I was an adult that I realized the song's biblical context.

These two introductions led me to brush Ecclesiastes aside as irrelevant to my spiritual life and failed to prepare me for the impact and impression it would eventually have on me. Despite the Reader's Digest Family Guide to the Bible verdict that it was "deeply pessimistic," I found Ecclesiastes an eminently practical book.

---

2 The Byrds. *Turn, Turn, Turn* (Turn, Turn, Turn, Columbia Records), 1965.

Borrowed Title

One of the first things I learned, especially as I delved into commentary after commentary, was the controversy over Ecclesiastes' authorship. Borrowing its title from the Septuagint—Ecclesiastes is the Latin translation of the Greek word for "church"—the actual Hebrew title is *Koholeth*, or "Words of the Preacher," and there's still debate over who, or what, the Preacher was.

Internal evidence, which places the composition around the ninth century B.C., seems to point to Solomon, making Ecclesiastes one of the three books of the Bible the third king of Israel supposedly wrote. The first was Song of Songs, a love song to one of his wives, written as a young man when Solomon was in the throes of true love. His description of the intimacies of physical love is unparalleled in scripture. His symbolic representation of this love to our relationship with God is unsurpassed.

Proverbs was Solomon's second book, written during his middle age. Many scholars suggest Proverbs was written at the height of Solomon's kingly power, when his reputation for wisdom had spread as far as Sheba, or modern–day Ethiopa (leading to the Queen of Sheba's royal visit to Ancient Israel).

Internal evidence also suggests that Ecclesiastes was written during Solomon's old age. Solomon had long since lost the intimate love he had once described. He had risen to power, been given riches beyond measure, and found all of it inadequate. Ecclesiastes is the ruminations of a cynical old man who once had everything—including a growing, maturing relationship with God. Solomon's selfishness and political expediency left him wanting:

> I, the Teacher, was king over Israel in Jerusalem. (Ecclesiastes 1:12)

> I undertook great projects… I bought male and female slaves and had other slaves who were born in my house. I also owned more herds and flocks than anyone in Jerusalem did before me. I amassed silver and gold for myself, and the treasure of kings and provinces… I became greater by far than anyone in Jerusalem before me. (Ecclesiastes

2:4, 8–9)

Other scholars suggest the Solomonic references were included by the anonymous author to make the work a pseudepigraph—a work in which the author hides his identity beneath that of some worthy ancient notable. These scholars, due to some of the grammatical, philosophical, and theological content, place the composition between the fifth and second centuries B.C.

Some may consider the answer to the question "Who wrote Ecclesiastes?" one that needs to be answered. The more I studied and delved into the debate, the more I came to the conclusion that the question of its authorship—whether it was by Solomon in the ninth century B.C. or an anonymous Teacher four to seven centuries later—was less important than the simple fact that it was included in the canon of Scripture. The author, who I'll refer to as the Teacher unless a reference to Solomon is warranted, makes observations that reverberate with and echo our twenty–first century experiences. The Teacher, this Everyman, succinctly described—and still describes—my own queries about life, many of which you'll read about in the following pages.

Three Themes

So how does Ecclesiastes resonate with today's reader? When I began studying Ecclesiastes in the 1990s, our society was faced with a period of economic unrest even though some economists suggested the economy rebounded and stabilized in the latter part of the decade. As we entered a new millennium, many at the lower end of the financial spectrum still searched for meaning, pounding the pavement in fruitless job searches. Bemoaning their lack of physical possessions, they also felt an unyielding thirst for spiritual fulfillment.

More than a decade later, not much has changed. The economy crashed again. People lost their jobs, houses, and material possessions. Many are spiritually thirsty but still distrust organized religion.

Into this atmosphere of unrest the Teacher gives us three key phrases: "meaningless," "under the sun," and "chasing the wind." This book will explore these themes and the Teacher's specific observations about them. We will examine the meaninglessness of wisdom, wishes, and work; the futility—or chasing the wind—of desire and deeds; and the eternal and temporal curses and joys of toil, treasures, and termination.

As pessimistic as Ecclesiastes seems, the Teacher leaves us with hope. Only once we've chased after the wind and become weary of the meaninglessness found under the sun do we come to the end of the matter.

Discussion Questions

Focus

1. When have you, like Spock, found that having is not, after all, so satisfying a thing as wanting?

Zoom In

2. If you've read Ecclesiastes before, what were your impressions of it? What's kept you from reading it before?

3. *"I see that all effort and all achievement springs from men's mutual jealousy. This, too, is vanity and chasing of the wind"* (Ecclesiastes 4:4).—What does this verse say to you?

Develop

4. Why is Ecclesiastes important to study today? What do you hope to get from an understanding of this book?

PART ONE

Meaningless, Meaningless

1

WISDOM

To the man who pleases him, God gives wisdom, knowledge and happiness, but to the sinner he gives the task of gathering and storing up wealth to hand it over to the one who pleases God. This too is meaningless, a chasing after the wind.
(Ecclesiastes 2:26)

My mother loved assembling jigsaw puzzles. She began with the smaller fifty to one hundred piece puzzles of pastoral scenery and eventually graduated to the larger five hundred to one thousand–plus piece puzzles. She especially enjoyed puzzles with scenes reflected in a lake or a river because it added an extra challenge: was the piece she had in hand part of the scene or part of the reflection?

Mom had a particular method of putting the puzzle together. She meticulously separated the pieces according to color. She also set aside the edge pieces. She began with the edges, creating a framework with which to work.

Every once in a while she would become frustrated. Often a piece would go missing, especially along the edge, resulting in a search among the other piles. Or one of the middle pieces would have been deceivingly cut to make it appear to be an edge piece. After trying to fit or force it into place, Mom would have to set it aside for future reference.

Wisdom is like a jigsaw puzzle, suggests the Teacher; just when it looks like all the pieces are falling into place, along comes a piece that doesn't fit. The Teacher writes, in Ecclesiastes' first chapter:

> I thought to myself, "Look, I have grown and increased in wisdom more than anyone who has ruled over Jerusalem before me; I have

> experienced much of wisdom and knowledge." Then I applied myself to the understanding of wisdom, and also of madness and folly, but I learned that this, too, is a chasing after the wind. For with much wisdom comes much sorrow; the more knowledge, the more grief. (Ecclesiastes 1:16–18)

In this passage—one that suggests Solomon's authorship—we wonder why the man reputed for his outstanding wisdom bemoans the experience of wisdom and knowledge.

The most popular example of Solomonic wisdom concerns two prostitutes who give birth to baby boys who are just days apart. During the night, one of the infants dies. One of the mothers switches the babies, insisting the live child is hers. The other woman makes the same claim. Solomon proposes to cut the child in half so each would have a share. Motherly love fills the woman whose son is still alive. "Don't kill him," she cries, preferring a live son raised by a false mother than half a dead son. Solomon wisely discerns her motherly love and returns the baby to his true mother.

The Queen of Sheba once made a perilous journey to Israel in order to test Solomon's wisdom. Kings and queens of the known world often sent envoys from their nations to learn from Solomon's wisdom.

Heavy, though, is the weight of wisdom.

> To the man who pleases him, God gives wisdom, knowledge and happiness, but to the sinner he gives the task of gathering and storing up wealth to hand it over to the one who pleases God. This too is meaningless, a chasing after the wind. (Ecclesiastes 2:26)

Solomon's wisdom was a gift from God. As his kingly reign began, Solomon spent time in prayer and sacrifice at Gibeon. God, appearing in a dream, asked Solomon what he wanted. Solomon asked for a discerning heart—so he could govern the Israelites properly by distinguishing right from wrong. God granted Solomon's request. Since Solomon did not ask for fame and fortune, God gave him that as well.

Solomon, however, squandered his relationship with God. *"As Solomon grew old, his wives turned his heart after other gods, and his heart was not fully devoted to the Lord his God, as the heart of David his father had been"* (1 Kings 11:4). David may have sinned. David may have committed adultery, conspired to commit murder, and taken a census when he shouldn't have, but he never abandoned God. Solomon didn't repeat the sins of his father, but he did abandon God.

Solomon bemoaned his wisdom because he knew it was a gift from God. He knew it was his responsibility to be a steward of that wisdom. Solomon wasted this gift by throwing away his relationship with God.

The Concise Oxford Dictionary defines a steward as a "person entrusted with management of another's property."[3] The word "steward" is derived from an Old English word which spoke of

---

3 Sykes, J.B, ed. *The Concise Oxford Dictionary of Current English* (New York, NY: Oxford University Press, 1988), p. 1043.

the "hall ward,"[4] or one who guarded the house or hall. Good stewardship pleases God, as the first portion of 2:26 declares: *"To the man who pleases him, God gives wisdom, knowledge and happiness."* Good stewardship recognizes that we, in the midst of God's creation, are entrusted with time, talents, and treasure. For Solomon, stewardship required him to continually recognize that his wisdom was from God and that it had to be used prudently, wisely.

When we recognize our stewardship responsibility—when we recognize that we are administrators, caretakers, agents, or custodians of our time, talent, and treasure—we are spurred into action. We use our God-given gifts to build up the body of Christ.

If we fail to recognize our responsibilities as stewards, or, as in Solomon's case, fail to maintain an intimate relationship with God, we run the risk of losing the benefits of God's gifts: *"To the sinner he gives the task of gathering and storing up wealth to hand it over to the one who pleases God"* (Ecclesiastes 2:26).

---

4 Ibid.

Jesus reinforced this thought with his parable of the talents. A master, before leaving for a journey, gave one servant five talents, another servant two talents, and a third servant one talent. The first two servants put their money to work and received a one hundred percent return for their efforts. The third servant buried his money. When the master returned, he praised the first two servants and gave them each additional responsibilities. The third servant was chastised for not even banking the money to gain interest.

Jesus laid out the parable's lesson clearly, reiterating the key teaching of Ecclesiastes:

> Take the talent from him and give it to the one who has the ten talents. For everyone who has will be given more, and he will have an abundance. Whoever does not have, even what he has will be taken from him. (Matthew 25:28–29)

Wisdom can be a puzzle. My mom often tried to fit pieces where they didn't belong. And she often searched the floor and table for missing pieces.

With the picture on the box, Mom put the pieces in the right places. Being skillful stewards of the wisdom God has given us—seeing the picture of stewardship from God's perspective—will help us put the pieces of life in the right place.

Solomon failed, seeing wisdom as meaningless, because he lost sight of the big picture. God has given us Solomon's words and wisdom so that we can learn from his mistakes.

If we don't, our gifts will become meaningless.

Discussion Questions

Focus

1. Do you think wisdom is like a jigsaw puzzle? Why, or why not?

Zoom In

2. How did Solomon lose his wisdom? How can abandoning God lead to a loss of wisdom?

3. Have you squandered your God–given gifts? How? Why?

Develop

4. How can you be a better steward of your time, talents, and treasure?

2

WISHES

Enjoy what you have rather than desiring what you don't have. Just dreaming about nice things is meaningless; it is like chasing the wind.
(Ecclesiastes 6:9, NLT)

The fisherman and his wife lived in a shabby sea shanty. Simple surroundings, a dry dinghy, and copious catches took care of the fisherman's wants and needs.

His wife's wants were more worldly.

One day the fisherman caught a talking fish, who told the tale of an enchanted prince. The fisherman, as compassionate as he was poor, threw the fish back into the ocean. At day's end, he related the tale to his wife, expecting praise for his pains.

"You fool!" she bellowed. "The least you could have done was demand a wish from the fish for sparing his life. Tomorrow you must return to where you found the fish, call for it, and ask that our shanty be turned into a cottage."

The next day, the fisherman returned to the sea and called for the fish, doubting such a small fish would hear his words in such a large ocean. To his surprise, the fish replied and granted the wish. Returning home, the fisherman found a quaint, colourful cottage instead of the shanty.

Soon his wife tired of the cottage.

"You know, you really did that fish a favour sparing his life," she said. "It's worth more than a cottage. If he had been a prince, he would have lived in a castle. Should you not be worth that much to him?"

She demanded her husband seek the fish once more and ask him to exchange the cottage for a castle. Her husband obeyed, going out in search of the fish the following day. Still at sea, on his way into the harbour, he spied the gleaming spires of a castle in place of his cottage.

Week upon week, the wife's wishes were followed with a command to find the fish and ask for more. Each time, the husband obediently brought the request to the fish, and the grateful fish granted each one.

That is, until the day the wife demanded to be God. The fish refused. That evening, the fisherman returned home to a shabby sea shanty and a wife who wished she hadn't been so greedy.

Our desire for riches fuels many of our endeavours. But the Teacher stated, *"All people spend their lives scratching for food, but they never seem to have enough"* (Ecclesiastes 6:7, NLT).

If we assume that Solomon authored Ecclesiastes, this passage takes on added significance. In addition to being rich in wisdom, Solomon was rich in material possessions:

- Each day his household of five thousand consumed one hundred and eighty–five bushels of wheat, three hundred and seventy–five bushels of cornmeal, thirty cows, one hundred sheep and goats, and numerous deer, gazelle, roebucks, and fowl.

- His annual income included twenty–five tons of gold in taxes from his kingdom, excise and tax revenue from merchants, traders, governors, and all the kings of Arabia.
- He furnished his forest palace in Lebanon with two hundred shields each made from fifteen pounds of gold and three hundred shields each made from four pounds of gold.
- Solomon had an ivory throne overlaid with pure gold.
- All of his drinking cups were solid gold, as were all the palace utensils.
- He had a fleet of trading ships, which would return from trade journeys with gold, silver, ivory, apes, and peacocks.

- Gifts from visiting royalty, dignitaries, and commoners included gold, silver, clothing, weapons, spices, horses, and mules.

Solomon wanted for little. Most of us would be satisfied with too much money at the end of the month rather than the usual too much month at the end of the money. In looking at the wealth of one like Solomon, the Teacher still has the audacity to state, *"The end of a man's toil is to fill his belly, yet his appetite is never satisfied."*

Wishing for wealth is meaningless, implies the Teacher. Even Solomon, living in the lap of luxury, realized the fleetingness of wealth.

The Teacher concludes, *"Enjoy what you have rather than desiring what you don't have. Just dreaming about nice things is meaningless; it is like chasing the wind"* (Ecclesiastes 6:9, NLT).

Similarly, Jesus stated:

> Can worry make you live longer? Why worry about clothes? Look how the wild flowers grow. They don't work hard to make their

clothes. But I tell you that Solomon with all his wealth wasn't as well clothed as one of them. God gives such beauty to everything that grows in the fields, even though it is here today and thrown into a fire tomorrow. He will surely do even more for you! Why do you have such little faith?

Don't worry and ask yourselves, "Will we have anything to eat? Will we have anything to drink? Will we have any clothes to wear?" Only people who don't know God are always worrying about such things. Your Father in heaven knows that you need all of these. But more than anything else, put God's work first and do what he wants. Then the other things will be yours as well.

Don't worry about tomorrow. It will take care of itself. You have

> enough to worry about today. (Matthew 6:27–34, CEV)

Some versions of Matthew 6:27 include the question, “Can worry add a foot to your height?” This translation has particular meaning to one such as me, who is vertically challenged. Despite my best efforts, I still haven’t been able to worry myself into a 5’6” frame. As an adolescent, I still paid the child’s admission rate at the Canadian National Exhibition. I always stumped the “guess your age” guy on the midway. My height, or lack thereof, caused considerable difficulty when I did try to get into an age–related event or activity. Showing a driver’s license, university ID, or age of consent card led to the inevitable suspicion that I was presenting a fake. Depending on the situation, either a temper tantrum or a puppy–dog look would evoke enough fear or sympathy for me to be let in—but usually with a warning that if they discovered I wasn’t as old as I said, I’d never be allowed in again.

The richest person I have ever known is my friend Daniel. When I met Daniel, he was living in the basement suite of his family home, which he’d inherited from his mother. He rented out the main floor and worked a variety of odd jobs. He never seemed to have a steady, full–time job, compared to me, who worked in the advertising department of a daily newspaper with my sights set on becoming a reporter. His freedom from the nine to five grind gave him numerous ministry opportunities, including leading nursing home services, disk jockeying at a Christian roller–skating rink, one–on–one counselling, etc.

Daniel never seemed to lack for faith, friends, or finances. His material wealth was miniscule in comparison to Solomon's. But his faith in God's provision never wavered. Even after he married, he and his wife only seemed to seek out enough work to provide finances for their burgeoning puppet ministry.

All of the people in this chapter—the fisherman, his wife, Solomon, and Daniel—had material needs. We all have material needs. But as the Teacher has reminded us, we have to put those needs in a proper perspective. While the fisherman's sea shanty may not have been appropriate to his needs, the cottage was probably more suitable than the castle.

God told Solomon that his choice of wisdom over wealth would bring him both wisdom and wealth. But much of Solomon's wealth was unnecessary and resulted from the heavy taxation of his subjects. Solomon's greed ultimately resulted in a split between Israel and Judah, which occurred when Solomon's son Rehoboam refused to relieve his father's taxation policy.

My friend Daniel had God's grasp on material possessions—don't worry about them, trust in God's provision, make God's will paramount, and everything you need will be provided.

Discussion Questions

Focus

1. What do you wish for? Why?

Zoom In

2. Why, after talking about Solomon's wealth, did the teacher say, "*The end of a man's toil is to fill his belly, yet his appetite is never satisfied?*"

3. How do you enjoy what you have instead of wishing for what you don't have?

Develop

4. How do you put your needs in a proper perspective?

3

WORK

I hated all the things I had toiled for under the sun, because I must leave them to the one who comes after me. And who knows whether he will be a wise man or a fool? Yet he will have control over all the work into which I have poured my effort and skill under the sun. This too is meaningless.
(Ecclesiastes 2:18–19)

As the host of the Discovery Channel show *Dirty Jobs*, Mike Rowe's job is to get dirty, yucky, and messy. Discovery Channel's website[5] describes the show this way:

5 www.dsc.discovery.com

> "Dirty Jobs" profiles the unsung American labourers who make their living in the most unthinkable—yet vital—ways. Our brave host and apprentice Mike Rowe will introduce you to a hardworking group of men and women who overcome fear, danger and sometimes stench and overall ickiness to accomplish their daily tasks.

Since the show—which stars manual labour, blood, sweat, and what Rowe affectionately calls "poo"—started in 2005, Rowe has:

- Inspected a working sewer complete with rats and waste.
- Collected and examined owl vomit.
- Worked as a minor league baseball groundskeeper—where the former opera singer ended the show by singing the American national anthem before the game.

- Milked spiders for their venom.
- Helped make shark food for an aquarium in Las Vegas.

As "glamorous" as this may seem, Rowe's jobs have left their mark. In an interview with TV.com, he says:

> There is, however, a fairly long litany of infirmaries and minor injuries. I won't bore you with a list—it's long… In [a] coming season, the wear and tear will be more noticeable and you may notice the fruits of my dirty labors in the very visible shape of eye infections, pronounced limps and most recently, a missing tooth.[6]

Watching *Dirty Jobs* lets the viewer realize that no matter how bad their job may be—there could be one out there that's worse. As Rowe muses,

> It's surprising how many people come home from relatively "clean"

6 http://www.tv.com/mike–rowe/person/61054/trivia.html

> jobs at the end of the day feeling bitter and miserable. Whereas the people I meet, by and large, seem really content with their lives, and happy with their dirty jobs.[7]

Despite the injuries, muck, and poo, Rowe enjoys his dirty jobs. And so do many of us—for a time. While there is excitement in practically every job, there's also the mundane details that fill the bulk of the workday. As a reporter, I spent an evening on a ride–along with a small–town Alberta police officer who described his job as comprising "long periods of boredom punctuated with short periods of sheer terror."

For most of us, the nine to five grind is comprised of immensely long periods of boredom punctuated with extremely short periods of excitement. No matter how interesting our work is, there are still times when we wish there was more to our job than the mundane day–to–day tasks that take up the bulk of our time. As a reporter, I had my share of interesting activities: flying a glider, floating in a

7 Ibid.

hot air balloon, meeting and interviewing celebrities, and covering groundbreaking news stories. But the bulk of my time was spent tracking down leads, sitting in city or county council meetings, reading reports, phoning to set up interviews, driving around to find interesting photo opportunities, and typing submissions by local column writers.

As satisfied as we may be with our jobs, most of us eventually realize that we will leave that job. With statistics showing the average person changing jobs every three years, we've probably all wondered what the end result of our two, three, four or more decades of work will be. Each time I left a newspaper, I wondered if the reporter replacing me would be able to build on the trust relationships I had built with local politicians and civic leaders. Or I wondered if they would take a hard–nosed news approach and become an adversary to those leaders in order to obtain their information. When I left a lay ministry position with The Salvation Army in Kelowna, B.C., I wondered if any of the programs began during my tenure would survive. I was particularly fond of the food co–op program and was pleased when I hit the church's website a number of years later to see it was still in operation.

I think many of us agree with the Teacher when he says:

> I hated all the things I had toiled for under the sun, because I must leave them to the one who comes after me. And who knows whether he will be a wise man or a fool? Yet he will have control over all the work into which I have poured my effort and skill under the sun. This too is meaningless. (Ecclesiastes 2:18–19)

One reason we feel the daily grind pummels us into meaningless chaff is because we've forgotten for whom we work.

My first job was in the advertising department of a daily newspaper in Edmonton, Alberta. I was brash, strong–willed, and quick–tempered. One of my managers was just as brash, strong–willed, and quick–tempered. Our conversations were often peppered with self–centred anger, with each of us trying to prove the other wrong. I often found myself acquiescing to my superior, not because he was right, but because he was the boss—and he frequently reminded me of that fact.

Once I made an error that resulted in the wrong advertisement appearing for one of the paper's major customers. As soon as I saw the ad, I traced my steps, discovered the error, and explained it to the salesperson. In the midst of this conversation, the manager stormed into my work area and demanded to know what had happened.

"I made a mistake," I acknowledged.

The manager stood in the doorway dumbfounded and disbelieving, expecting more of an argument and ready to castigate me. My calm acceptance of the error floored him and he trudged away, mumbling, "Don't let it happen again."

Upon reflection, I realized this was one of the few times I, a professing Christian, really understood what it meant to put Christ first in the workplace. It's taken nearly two decades, but it's now easier to put what could be meaningless work into perspective: we do it by realizing that we ultimately do everything for God's glory.

Paul wrote:

> Slaves [or employees], obey your earthly masters in everything; and do it, not only when their eye is on you and to win their favor, but with sincerity of heart and reverence for the Lord. Whatever you do, work at it with all your heart, as working for the Lord, not for men. (Colossians 3:22–23)

Employers or fellow employees won't bring meaning to work. A competent boss who understands how to meld Christian ethics with effective management techniques will make a job easier. Working with a team of capable and compassionate fellow employees will make even the most mundane tasks seem a joy. Ultimately, though, our attitude will determine how enjoyable our work becomes.

We can, as the Teacher did, regret that all we work for might end up destroyed by those following in our footsteps. We can see our work solely as being the means by which we provide for our material needs. Or we can, as Paul instructed, work for the Lord. We can see our work as a ministry, no matter how far removed from the pulpit it seems. A plumber who snakes out a clogged toilet with a sincere heart and reverence for God is as much a minister as the evangelist whose sermons convince thousands to turn from a life of sin to a life of following God. A pastor who preaches because he wants people to think he's a great preacher is akin to a factory worker who can't wait for the whistle to blow at the end of the day, and for retirement at sixty–five; his ministry will be small.

Our work can be as meaningless or as meaningful as we want it to be. It all depends on whom we seek approval from—God or others.

Discussion Questions

Focus

1. How would you describe your job? Is it always exciting or is it tedious with brief moments of sheer terror?

Zoom In

2. Who is your boss?

3. Do you worry about what will happen to your work when you're gone?

Develop

4. Is your work meaningful? What will bring more meaning to your work?

PART TWO

Chasing the Wind

4

DESIRE

I have seen all the works which have been done under the sun, and behold, all is vanity and striving after wind.
(Ecclesiastes 1:14, NASB)

The battery–powered rabbit keeps on going and going and going, with the exception of a competitor's commercial where the rabbit is outrun by a competitor–powered turtle in parody of Aesop's famous fable.

But both the tortoise and the hare are only as good as their batteries. Their well–being is totally in the control of the cases of chemicals and compounds that help them operate. Despite their desire to be first all the time, their efficiency will eventually give way to the first law of thermodynamics—left to itself, a system will eventually decay into chaos.

Desire is a powerful motivator. Where would the automotive industry be without Henry Ford's desire to reduce the cost of assembling a car? Ford didn't invent the automobile or the assembly system. But his desire for efficiency, and for fame and fortune, motivated Ford to perfect the assembly line, which revolutionized not only the auto industry but many other industries as well.

We would still be in the dark if it weren't for Thomas Edison's desire to create the incandescent light. Night after night he experimented with different fabrics to create the perfect light bulb. Edison was once asked, after hundreds of experiments, if he was discouraged because he had so many failures. He replied that he wasn't discouraged; in fact, he was encouraged because he now knew the hundreds of methods that didn't work.

Desire, however, is often not enough to bring success.

Roger Bannister and John Landy both desired

to run the world's fastest mile. Both held that distinction when they met for the 1954 British Empire Games (now the Commonwealth Games) in Vancouver, B.C. A lasting image from that race has been immortalized in bronze at the gates of the Pacific National Exhibition grounds, where the race was held. Rounding the corner in the final stretch, the leading Landy looks behind him, to his left, only to be passed on the right by a surging Bannister, who won the race. Sports pundits have speculated through the years that if Landy hadn't looked back, he probably would have won the race.

Landy's desire to win wasn't enough. The backward glance, trying to determine where Bannister was, may have been born of fear—fear that Bannister was too close—or born of pride—pride that he was in the lead. Whatever Landy's reason for looking back, it created the hesitancy that allowed Bannister to surge ahead for the win.

We all have desires. Perhaps not the desires of a Ford, an Edison, a Bannister, or a Landy. Our desires are often simpler. We desire children who behave in public, a car that starts on a freezing winter day, a pay cheque that covers the bills, and a boss who commends us for our latest successful project. Often, though, our desires go unfulfilled: the children act like monsters, the muffler falls off the car as we back out of the driveway, our cash flow dries up to a trickle, and the boss bawls us out for something that isn't even our fault.

We begin to see the truth in the Teacher's words: *"I have seen all the things that are done under the sun; all of them are meaningless, a chasing after the wind"* (Ecclesiastes 1:14). The New American Standard Bible translates this verse as, *"I have seen all the works which have been done under the sun, and behold, all is vanity and striving after wind"* (NASB).

The word "striving" depicts an element of force, an element of dissatisfaction. An element of desire. Isn't it true that when we desire something—think of Ford, Edison, Bannister, and Landy—we strive to obtain the object of our desire? And unlike our examples, what we strive for or desire is generally devoid of meaning.

Possessions, prestige, and popularity are often foremost in our desires. This can be seen in a recent television trend—reality television. The first of the

American reality TV shows was *Survivor*. The show's premise was to drop sixteen people onto a tropical island and film them while they whittled away at each other as one person outwitted, outplayed, and outlasted all the others. The sixteen players, initially split up into two teams of eight, needed to overcome personal differences and distrust towards the others. Personal prejudices were put aside to build an effective team. Teamwork came into play during the weekly challenges that pitted one tribe against the other. The winning team gained immunity from voting one of their team members into TV oblivion.

The fly in the teamwork ointment is the prize. Each castaway's sense of self–preservation is working overtime so he or she can win the pot of gold at the end of the rainforest walk. The machinations taking place would make Machiavelli proud, whose seminal work, *The Prince*, describes the most effective ways of manipulating people to one's own advantage.

Viewing these self–centered manoeuvrings can make Christians feel smug in their ecclesiastical cocoon. But before we look at the specks in their eyes, we need to look at the palm branch in our own eyes.

Too often churches play their own game of *Survivor*, most often with the church board on one team, the pastor and/or his staff on the opposing team, and the congregation caught in the middle. It becomes a tug of war fraught with head and spy games that would make CIA agents jealous.

I've witnessed and been part of the survivors' games played out in church boardrooms, where alliances are formed with the intent of winning a prize—which can be as essential as choosing a pastor or as inconsequential as choosing the carpet color.

The desire to be the most important, to be the most powerful, or to have the most stuff is often overwhelming. We are humans and not plaster saints. But as those who have accepted God's call to serve him within the church, we need to move beyond survivor–like tactics. The Apostle Paul took the whole of his first letter to the church in Corinth to address this issue: *"You are still worldly. For since there is jealousy and quarreling among you, are you not worldly? Are you not acting like mere men?"*

(1 Corinthians 3:3)

Using the body as an example, Paul demonstrated how the whole is greater than the individual parts:

> But in fact God has arranged the parts in the body, every one of them, just as he wanted them to be. If they were all one part, where would the body be? As it is, there are many parts, but one body. (1 Corinthians 12:18–19)

The human foibles of pride and selfish gain became more and more evident as *Survivor* unfolded. God gives us the gifts of humility and selfless love, which ought to be more evident in the fellowship of believers.

Possession, position, and prestige are harmless in and of themselves. It's our desire for these things and what we do to obtain them that can create problems. Henry Ford, in his desire for these three Ps, became ruthless. When his workers went on strike for better wages and working conditions, he hired thugs to break up the strikes. He fired the organizers. He almost destroyed the company when his sons suggested changes to the Model–T in order to keep up with the times—for a time his competitors at General Motors were more successful than Ford. When it was suggested Ford add color to the cars, Henry Ford was heard to reply that customers could have their Ford in any color they wanted, as long as it was black.

Striving after (or desiring) possession, position, and prestige is like chasing the wind. If we seek them, they will always be beyond our grasp, as dust in the wind. Godly desire, the striving after God's will and seeking to build his kingdom, will always remain within our grasp. Solomon, when given the chance, didn't ask God for possessions, position, or prestige. Instead Solomon asked God to make him a wise ruler, one who could discern between right and wrong. This godly desire led to possessions, prestige, and position. God said:

> Solomon, I'm pleased that you asked for this. You could have asked to live a long time or to be rich. Or you could have asked for your enemies to be destroyed. Instead,

> you asked for wisdom to make right decisions. So I'll make you wiser than anyone who has ever lived or ever will live.
>
> I'll also give you what you didn't ask for. You'll be rich and respected as long as you live, and you'll be greater than any other king. If you obey me and follow my commands, as your father David did, I'll let you live a long time. (1 Kings 3:10–14, CEV).

Desire, in the case of Henry Ford, Thomas Edison, and Roger Bannister, resulted in great achievements. But desire can result in vain striving for goals we will never reach, as in the case of Landy. Solomon, though, sought the godly desire of wisdom and found himself rewarded beyond measure—an example we would be wise to follow.

Discussion Questions

Focus

1. What's been your greatest desire? What's stopped you from fulfilling that desire?

Zoom In

2. How do we move beyond our self–centred desires?

3. How can we move from being "plaster saints" to "human beings?"

Develop

4. How do we develop a godly perspective on the desire for possession, position, and prestige?

5

DEEDS

There is something else meaningless that occurs on earth: righteous men who get what the wicked deserve, and wicked men who get what the righteous deserve. This too, I say, is meaningless.
(Ecclesiastes 8:14)

It seems as if the warranty on my body ran out as I approached my fortieth birthday.

At least twice that year, I ended up in the emergency room with a burning in my right side as my undersized kidney battled infection. One such skirmish began as I was in a Bible college classroom in Toronto, almost two hours away from my home in Guelph. I still don't remember how I drove home that night, but I remember my ashen gray complexion as I waited in the doctor's office and hospital emergency room. A cocktail of antibiotics, ibuprofen, and a cranberry juice–ginger ale concoction helped flush the pain and infections from my system.

My body's rebellion continued as my fortieth year approached the halfway mark. Sitting in my office, talking on the phone, I suddenly blacked out. As I came to, bent over in my chair, a voice coming from the phone, I realized all was not well with my world. I hung up the phone, turned off the computer, and had a staff member drive me to the hospital while another picked up my wife Pam at home. At the hospital, it was discovered that my body's internal pacemakers had suffered a communication breakdown. The only solution was a pacemaker implant. Further investigation of my heart revealed that one of the valves, which had been repaired during surgery when I was a youth to correct a congenital heart condition, had become leaky and had to be replaced about a year later.

In the years that followed, I've seen my health

deteriorate, my employment situation change drastically, and my wife and children cope with innumerable pressures. This has caused me to become introspective. Taking the time to examine my life shines a spotlight on the changes God needs to effect in me.

I've also pondered the fate of others I've known. Men like Jim and Doug.

Jim loved life, and as a head elder and Sunday school teacher he lived it to the fullest. When two congregations amalgamated to form our church, it pleased me to hear that Jim would remain on as head elder, with his grace, peace, and spiritual maturity bringing stability to the new congregation. As a business owner, Jim's ethics were above reproach. He was rarely without a smile (at least I never saw him without one) and was a living example of what it meant to know Christ and make Him known. Jim's five decades on this earth were cut short when, while shovelling snow at the home he had built, he died of a heart attack.

Doug was active in men's groups and the spark plug of many men's camp activities. Another living example Jesus' love and life, Doug's life was also snuffed out after a brave battle with cancer. When I read the tribute to Doug's life in *The War Cry*, the Salvation Army's denominational magazine, I remembered his smiling face, off–key voice, and hearty handshake.

When I consider the wear and tear on my body, the premature deaths—from our perspective—of Jim and Doug, I think of the Teacher's words: *"There is something else meaningless that occurs on earth: righteous men who get what the wicked deserve, and wicked men who get what the righteous deserve. This too, I say, is meaningless"* (Ecclesiastes 8:14). This sentiment is best summed up in the title of a bestselling book from the mid–1980s—*Why Do Bad Things Happen to Good People?*

The Psalmist Asaph asked a similar question. He said:

> For I envied the arrogant [and] I saw the prosperity of the wicked. They have no struggles; their bodies are healthy and strong. They are free from the burdens common to man; they are not plagued by human ills. (Psalm 73:3–5)

Asaph admitted that by envying the evil his *"feet had almost slipped; [he] had nearly lost [his] foothold"* (Psalm 73:2). The more I considered the circumstances of my life in my early forties, the easier it was to begin to slip spiritually. It wasn't anything deliberate, like suddenly standing up in church Sunday morning and renouncing God. It was much more indirect, like finding excuses for not spending time in Bible study, allowing Internet surfing to take the place of prayer, or watching the lunchtime news rather than make the noon hour a time of devotion with my wife. The mountain was crumbling under my feet and my hands were tired of gripping the rocky handholds. I complained, along with Asaph, *"Surely in vain have I kept my heart pure; in vain have I washed my hands in innocence. All day long I have been plagued; I have been punished every morning"* (Psalm 73:13–14).

The Teacher, Asaph, and I only view life from one perspective. There are times when probing life from another perspective is needed.

I have been involved with Scouts Canada for decades. One of the movement's joys is the creation of a person's campfire blanket. Onto my blanket has been sewn crests representing various activities and events. Some crests date back to my days as a Cub more than forty years ago. My most treasured crests were the result of trades with the other members of a three–weekend training session.

If you were to look at the back of some of these finely embroidered crests, underneath the rubber coating you would find a tangle of loose threads. Even a glance at the back of my campfire blanket would reveal knots, loose threads, and tangles.

The Teacher, Asaph, and I need a new perspective. In Asaph's words, *"When I tried to understand all this, it was oppressive to me till I entered the sanctuary of God; then I understood their final destiny"* (Psalm 73:16–17). It's only when we look at the front of the crests or the blanket as a whole that we see the beautiful designs. It's only when we try to view life from God's perspective that we can live with the perceived injustices of life.

My pacemaker implant and leaky valve were the results of a congenital heart condition. The doctors never discovered a reason for my kidney infections.

But I've stopped wondering, "Why me?" The

slippery slope has given way to solid ground. The handholds are a little more comfortable and the footholds have stopped crumbling. I still question some of the world's injustices, but I've learned that I'm still only viewing the campfire blanket from the back. I keep waiting for the day it will be turned over so I can view its beauty from the front.

I just hope it isn't any time soon.

Discussion Questions

Focus

1. What are the circumstances in your life that have caused you to be introspective?

Zoom In

2. Asaph said that he "envied the evil" because they didn't seem to have any trouble. Have you ever felt this way? When? Why?

3. Have you been so discouraged by the success of those you think don't deserve it that you've nearly lost your foothold?

Develop

4. How easy is it to view life from God's perspective? What stops us from doing so? What can we do to view life from God's perspective?

PART THREE

Under the Sun

6

TOIL

Whoever watches the wind will not plant;
whoever looks to the clouds will not reap.
(Ecclesiastes 11:4)

While working for a newspaper in a small Alberta farming community, one of the locals told me I only needed to know four things to understand farming: "too hot, too cold, too wet, too dry."

However, I soon learned farming is more than weather conditions. Economics and politics are key elements in the farming community. A rally during an election campaign in that same town turned into a protest as disgruntled farmers literally drove home their disapproval of the government's economic policies—a protest of tractors drove into town during a rally featuring the provincial premier.

Endless arguments about economic policy are moot if farmers fail to plant their crops. A friend of mine who grew up on a Saskatchewan farm once told me one of his father's favourite sayings: "You can't grow if you don't sow." This adage echoes the Teacher's musings, made more pointedly in the New Living Translation: *"If you wait for perfect conditions, you will never get anything done"* (Ecclesiastes 11:4, NLT).

The Teacher's words make more sense when we consider farming techniques in the ancient Middle East. A farmer had to hitch his team of oxen to a plough in order to dig the furrows. Then, by hand, he scattered the seed into the furrows before covering them with soil. When the harvest was ready, he used hand scythes and winnows to cut the grain and separate the wheat from the chaff.

All this was made more difficult by the weather. Again, recalling my days in rural Alberta, there were times when town council meetings were cancelled during the planting and harvesting season if a stretch of poor weather broke. These modern–day farmers had to make the best of every opportunity to get their crops either into the ground or into the barn.

An Old Testament farmer, without the benefit of modern machinery, needed to be an even better steward of his time in order to ensure he had a crop that would take care of his family. He couldn't be, as the Teacher suggested, someone who spent more time second–guessing the weather than farming. A farmer who spent considerable time watching the wind at planting time, trying to decide if that day's wind would scatter the seed too much, might end up planting nothing at all. Taking the time to watch gathering storm clouds, or what could develop into storm clouds, might delay the harvest. A farmer who waited too long for a calm day to sow his seed might never plant a crop. A farmer who waited for threatening weather to pass might end up with a less than perfect crop, if a crop was harvested at all.

The best farmers, at least of those I've met, are those who wisely discern the signs and act when the conditions seem as perfect as possible.

How many of us toil over our decisions with a similar attitude? In the Matthew Henry Commentary, the author says, "If we stand thus magnifying every little difficulty, starting objections and fancying hardship where there is none, we shall never go on with our work."[8]

The Teacher is telling us to step out in faith. If God is leading us in a specific direction, we need to be obedient.

Like Abraham.

Abraham, or Abram as he was then known, was minding his own business in his home in Haran—until God told him to pack up his household, gather his family and servants, and move.

"I want you to move somewhere, but you won't know where that somewhere is until I tell you that you're at that somewhere," is a loose translation of Abram's transfer order. At the age of seventy–five, beyond what most of us consider retirement age, Abram listened to God, packed everything and everybody, and headed west until he reached

---

8 Henry, Matthew. *Matthew Henry's Commentary on the Bible* (Peabody, MA: Hendrickson Publishers), 1997. From Nelson's Electronic Bible Reference Library version.

Canaan, the Promised Land.

While the Promised Land was supposed to flow with milk and honey, following God's promises wasn't all peaches and cream for Abram. Because of a famine Abram was forced to move to the more bountiful Egypt where he got himself into trouble with the Pharaoh after trying to pass his wife off as his sister. An argument—after Abram's return to Canaan—with his nephew Lot, who thought he was getting a rough deal over property rights, meant Abram got stuck with the hill country while Lot took over the lush plain.

Eventually Abram, tired of waiting for God's promised heir, took matters into his own hands, got his wife's maid pregnant and, when the baby came, threw the maid and infant out into the desert. When Abram finally did have a legitimate son with his wife, God asked him, as a test of his faith, to sacrifice that preadolescent son, Isaac. A test Abram passed.

It's possible that Abraham wasn't prepared for any of these tasks. He certainly wasn't prepared for the argument with Lot. If Abraham was like any father I know, he certainly wasn't prepared to sacrifice Isaac. If, paraphrasing the words of the Teacher, Abraham had waited for perfect conditions, he wouldn't have gotten anything done. His move to Canaan was made at an inopportune time; he was settled in Haran and seemed too old for another major move. If Abraham had waited, he never would have left. If he had waited for the perfect conditions to sacrifice Isaac, he would have failed God's test of faith.

In the one instance when Abraham should have waited for the perfect conditions—or, more to the point, God's conditions—Abraham blew it. For a number of years, decades actually, Abraham had been waiting for God to fulfill His promise of blessing him with descendants as numerous as the stars. But Sarah aged childless, well beyond her childbearing years. Abraham realized his chance to be a father was fading as fast as camel tracks in the desert sand. Then Sarah had an idea. Although there was snow on Abraham's roof, the fire still burned in his furnace, so Sarah offered her maid, Hagar, as a surrogate. According to the common practice at the time, Hagar could bear a child, which, if a son, would become Abraham's heir and the beginning of the fulfillment of God's seemingly unfulfilled promise.

The plan went well until Sarah grew jealous of Hagar. While the scriptures are somewhat silent on the matter, we can speculate about the envy Sarah felt towards Hagar, who was able to deliver the son she couldn't. Hagar may have exhibited pride, turning the knife ever so slowly into Sarah's soul. Whatever took place between the women, Sarah finally had enough. She complained to Abraham, who tossed Hagar and her young son into the desert.

But God always keeps his promises. Ishmael was Abraham's seed and was destined to be the father of a nation. God delivered this message to Hagar and Ishmael became the father of the Ishmaelites, who were—and are—a thorn in the sides of Abraham's and Sarah's legitimate children.

The Teacher warned us about the consequences of waiting too long for perfect conditions. Abraham's actions remind us about the consequences of not waiting for God's conditions. Our salvation isn't dependent upon our works, or toil. But faith and works are the soul's two legs in our spiritual walk—first faith steps out, and then works, until each are striding rhythmically in a solid walk. In a sermon a long time ago, I once heard the comment that you need to work as if everything depends on you, and pray as if everything depends on God.

The Teacher couldn't have said it better.

Discussion Questions

Focus

1. What are you waiting for the perfect conditions to do? Are you second–guessing an important—or not–so–important—decision?

Zoom In

2. What would you do if God gave you the same direction as He did Abraham? Would you be as willing as Abraham to follow God's direction?

3. Have you become tired of waiting on God? What have you done to "hurry" God? How has that worked for you?

Develop

4. How can you develop a spiritual life that sees faith and works walking in rhythm? What can prevent you from creating such a walk of faith?

7

TREASURES

To the man who pleases him, God gives wisdom, knowledge and happiness, but to the sinner he gives the task of gathering and storing up wealth to hand it over to the one who pleases God…
(Ecclesiastes 2:26)

Jesus told the story of a manager who was caught with his hand in the till. When his boss asked him to account for the discretion, the manager began fearing for his job and future: *"I'm not strong enough to dig, and I'm ashamed to beg"* (Luke 16:3).

So the manager hatched a plan that would open doors for him. He began calling each of the people who owed his boss money, asking about their outstanding balances. For the one who owed the boss nine hundred gallons of olive oil, he cut the bill in half. For the one who owed one thousand bushels of wheat, he reduced it to eight hundred.

The boss finally caught wind of the scheme. Interestingly, instead of firing the manager, he praised him for being so shrewd and let him keep his job.

The lesson, suggested Jesus:

> Whoever can be trusted with very little can also be trusted with much, and whoever is dishonest with very little will also be dishonest with much. So if you have not been trustworthy in handling worldly wealth, who will trust you with true riches? (Luke 16:10–11)

The manager was praised for his shrewdness, not his honesty. Jesus suggests that God wants trustworthy and honest stewards, while the words of the Teacher—"*To the man who pleases him, God gives wisdom, knowledge and happiness*" (Ecclesiastes 2:26)—provides two further insights into God's view of stewardship:

- Wisdom, happiness, and knowledge are the good steward's reward.
- The small amount entrusted to a poor steward will be given to a wise steward.

Jesus' parable of the shrewd manager highlights an area of stewardship we often neglect: our employment. A pastor once shared with me a conversation he'd had with a leading employer in the community in which we lived. "Christians make the worst employees," the businessman told the pastor. The pastor heard complaints about the poor ethics of Christian employees who demonstrated unrealistic expectations, sloth, and poor work habits. The employer seriously considered no longer hiring anyone who used a minister as a reference.

Godly stewardship also extends to employers. A few years before this conversation, I'd heard comments from an employee about her Christian employer. She complained about lack of ethics, poor management skills, unrealistic expectations, and poor work habits.

Having spent more than two decades in the workforce, for both Christian and non–Christian employers, I can honestly say, in my experience, that a profession of Christian faith doesn't guarantee a perfect employer/employee relationship on either the employer's or employee's part. Some of my non–Christian bosses and fellow employees treated me better than certain Christians did. There have also been Christian employers and fellow employees who demonstrated a Christ–like grace, mercy, and patience that I had never before experienced. I also worked for and with Christians and non–Christians who were manipulative, impatient, and self–centred.

If in every area of our life, including the workplace, we exhibit good stewardship, the Teacher promises *"wisdom, happiness and knowledge."*

Stewardship can be a harsh taskmaster. If we misuse our time, talent, and treasure, it will be taken away from us. Our first responsibility is the recognition of God as the originator of our gifts.

A foolish farmer once failed to recognize God in this way. After a successful harvest, one that was so plentiful he needed to build newer and larger storage bins, the farmer took all the credit for the bounty. He forgot that God allows the sun and the rain to pour down on both the righteous and the unrighteous. The farmer forgot that while he planted the seed, it was God who provided the harvest.

The result? "Let's eat, drink, and be merry," boasted the farmer.

"You fool," God replied. "Tonight I require your soul."

How can we determine if we are good or bad stewards? How can we tell if we'll receive wisdom, knowledge, and happiness or have to hand over the little we have to one who pleases God? Perhaps some self–examination will assist us:

- Do we recognize the source of our gifts, which God has given us to use in our calling as employees and employers?
- Do we recognize our responsibility as stewards? Do we work as unto the Lord or do we do just enough to get by?

- Are we aware of how well we take care of the time, talent, and treasure God's given us? As employees and employers, do we see our jobs and careers as vocations that demand the best use of our time, talent, and treasure?
- Do we return a portion of our time, talents, and treasure to the God who has given it to us (commonly known as a tithe)? Do we see our jobs as the means by which God provides us with the resources to expand His kingdom?

As stewards, we can imitate the manager who kept his job by being shrewd instead of honest. Or we can imitate the farmer who failed to recognize God as the source of his bounty. Or we can emulate the stewards who recognized the source of their talents and used them to glorify God.

The choice is ours.

Discussion Questions

Focus

1. What kind of treasure has God entrusted you with? How have you used it?

Zoom In

2. How to we show good stewardship as employees? How do we show good stewardship as employers? How does this apply to the self–employed?

3. Do you think it's fair that God may take away the treasures of those who are poor stewards? Why? Why not?

Develop

4. What's one thing we can do to improve our stewardship of our vocations and our treasures?

8

TERMINATION

Remember him—before the silver cord is severed, or the golden bowl is broken; before the pitcher is shattered at the spring, or the wheel is broken at the well, and the dust returns to the ground it came from, and the spirit returns to God who gave it.
(Ecclesiastes 12:6–7)

Gingerly, hesitantly, I trudged towards the body. My cotton-gloved hands reached towards the cat's tail. My heart raced. My breakfast flip-flopped in my stomach. I bent over and picked up the frozen, rigid corpse. At arm's length, I placed it in the green plastic bag. The deed done, I took the steps needed to dispose of the body.

Why, I wondered, should the body of a dead cat found on my property bother me so much? Why should this stray feline, now scratching in the big litter box in the sky, have caused such a reaction?

Occasionally my wife and I will refer to what we've come to nickname the "New Year's cat" with gallow's humour. The more I think about my reaction as I disposed of the body, the more I realize the cat confronted me with my own mortality.

I've never found death easy to handle. On my inaugural visit to a hospitalized cancer patient, I froze. It was the first time in a number of months since I'd seen the woman, a member of the church where I was an elder. I was struck speechless and motionless by the sight of a body ravaged by cancer. Fortunately the friend who accompanied me was prepared and able to handle the situation.

Similar fears and feelings confronted me as I later watched my father die of liver cancer. Slowly the disease drained Dad of his vitality. Standing at his bedside, looking at his empty shell in an Edmonton hospital, waves of emotion overwhelmed me as I tried to make some sense of his death.

The fear of death affects many people. In his book *Unknown Gods,* sociologist Reg Bibby says that about fifteen percent of Canadians say dying concerns them "a great deal" or "quite a bit" while another thirty percent say it bothers them "somewhat."[9]

I realized the limits of my mortality when I underwent open–heart surgery in my early forties. My recollection of the days following the surgery are recorded in a journal:

> I experienced an overwhelming feeling of nothingness as I tried to figure out what day and time it was. I felt like I'd been through a war. My chest hurt. I got up twice in the night to go to the washroom only to find myself groggy, in pain, incoherent, and insufferable.

I derived some comfort from the material and counsel provided in the hospital which explained the normality of my experiences.

---

9 Bibby, Reginald W. *Unknown Gods* (Toronto, Canada: Stoddart Publishing, 1997).

Despite the inevitability of death, the Teacher provides some consolation: *"He has also set eternity in the hearts of men; yet they cannot fathom what God has done from beginning to end"* (Ecclesiastes 3:11).

Curiosity about our future, which also includes death, can be compared to a drive along the Columbia Icefields Parkway, which runs between Jasper and Banff National Parks. As you approach the boundary that separates the two parks, you drive up a steep, winding mountain road.

The drive can be somewhat disconcerting because it's impossible to know what lies beyond the next bend. A mountain blocks the view. You don't know if mountain goats have descended for a few licks of salt, or if a black bear has decided to sun itself along the side of the road. You don't even know if another driver, trying to stay away from the mountain's edge, has crossed the center line and strayed into your lane.

We can be as curious about our future as I was about what was beyond the next bend in the road. Life is filled with various seasons and events. The Teacher listed the most important: birth and death, planting and harvesting, killing and healing, tearing down and building up, weeping and laughing, mourning and dancing, scattering and gathering, embracing and standing back, tearing and mending, silence and speaking, loving and hating, and war and peace (Ecclesiastes 3:2–8). Curiosity about which season will follow the next, especially the season of death (specifically our own), derives from the God–given sense of eternity that has been set in our hearts.

Death and the future can indeed be frightening. Into this atmosphere of fear come the words of the Teacher: "They cannot fathom what God has done from beginning to end."

We cannot understand the workings of God. We don't have a crystal ball with which to see the future. Nor should we want to.

The New Year's cat story began on New Year's Eve one year, when we came back from our church's New Year's Eve social. The stray cat pleaded to be let into our warm home. Our compassion was tempered by the presence of our pet cat, Prissie, who brooked no rivals (even perceived rivals). There was no way of knowing what would greet us the next morning on the front lawn.

An active faith in the One who has set eternity in our hearts, in the God who gave us the spirit of life, diminishes our anxiety of death. The Apostle Paul described how the sting of death and victory of the grave was destroyed through Jesus' own death on the cross. But a natural anxiety arises for those of us facing the great unknown of the great beyond. The taste of termination may not be any less bitter, but the beckoning of death becomes less alarming to those who trust in the living God.

Discussion Questions

Focus

1. Why does death frighten people?

Zoom In

2. How does God “set eternity in our hearts”? If you could ask God about one circumstance in your life, what would it be?

3. Looking at the seasons of life in Ecclesiastes 3:2–8, what season of life are you in? What season would you prefer to be in?

Develop

4. How can we learn to trust God—even in the face of death?

THE END OF THE MATTER

Now all has been heard; here is the conclusion of the matter: Fear God and keep his commandments, for this is the whole duty of man.
(Ecclesiastes 12:13)

The Teacher deems wisdom, wishes, and work as meaningless.

Striving after desire and deeds is like chasing the wind.

The only constants under the sun are toil, treasure, and termination.

In the end, much of life seems to be futile and unattainable.

While reading Ecclesiastes, one wonders if the Teacher, after climbing the ladder of success, looked back on his life and realized the ladder leaned against the wrong wall.

In *The 7 Habits of Highly Effective People*, author Stephen Covey encourages his readers to imagine themselves at their own funerals, listening to the eulogy. Then he asks them to write the eulogy they want to hear. The exercise demonstrates the specific changes a person may have to make to ensure that the eulogy they want to hear is the one that is delivered.

This was the first step in self–improvement because, as Covey said, you "begin with the end in mind."[10] This principle, beginning with the end in mind, is as old as Ecclesiastes. The ending which the Teacher espouses is to *"fear God and keep his commandments"* (Ecclesiastes 12:13).

Wisdom, wishes, work, desires, deeds, toil, treasure, and termination are all desirable. The writer of Hebrews wrote:

---

10 Covey, Stephen R. *The 7 Habits of Highly Effective People* (New York, NY: Free Press, 2004), pp. 96–97.

> What God has said isn't only alive and active! It is sharper than any double–edged sword. His word can cut through our spirits and souls and through our joints and marrow, until it discovers the desires and thoughts of our hearts. (Hebrews 4:12, CEV)

The Teacher, with each of his observations, places that separating scimitar in our hands and hearts. All of these major themes have two possible outcomes: they can be used to serve self or they can be used to serve God.

Solomon, often thought to be the Teacher, initially viewed wisdom as meaningful—he chose wisdom over fame and fortune in the early days of his kingship. God gave Solomon more wisdom, along with fame and fortune, than Solomon had dreamed. But Solomon began to see the trees rather than the forest, losing sight of the "big picture." His final analysis was to deem wisdom as meaningless—but Solomon's lasting words, found in God's Word, are a warning to those of us who would squander our God–given wisdom.

The cliché "if wishes were horses, beggars would ride," while not biblical, has its roots in the words of the Teacher, who deemed wishes as meaningless. Too often our wishes are geared towards material prosperity—remember the fisherman and his wife? Greed, not need, fuels lottery fever and unethical business choices. Our choice is to either allow our wishes for prosperity to control our lives or to adopt God's perspective on possessions: trust in Him, make His will paramount, and everything we need will be provided.

Statisticians tell us that the average person will change his career at least three times. Which means the foundation we've built in one workplace may not last beyond our time in that position. The Teacher bemoaned this fact, that all we have worked for may end up being destroyed by those who follow in our footsteps. Our work can be seen solely as a way to pay the bills and buy the groceries. Or work can be perceived as a ministry. It can be as meaningful as we want it to be, especially if we do our work for God and not others.

Desire has resulted in great achievements. Henry Ford's desire to make the car affordable for the masses resulted in an improved assembly line. Roger Bannister's desire to run the fastest mile led to his victory over John Landy. Even the most self-centred desires can result in good. But godly desires—the desire to love mercy, do justly, and walk humbly before God, for example—will result in more than good. Godly desires will lead to justice and holy living.

Cub Scouts promise to "do a good deed every day." But often the deeds of others, even the deeds of God, can leave us wondering, "Why me?" My health, or lack thereof, left me with many questions. The injustices in the world, such as the 9/11 terrorist attacks in 2001, also leave us with questions for God. But like a tapestry viewed from the back, all we see are the knots and tangles of deeds done and undone, not the beautiful picture on the front. Our choice is to keep wondering what the picture is, or to trust that the deeds of God—when viewed from His perspective—will create a beautiful tapestry.

Timing is the key to toiling well. The Teacher told us that waiting too long for perfect conditions would lead to dire consequences. Abraham's actions are reminders of the consequences of not waiting for God's conditions. We can either toil away on our own or recognize that faith and works are the two legs of the soul in our spiritual walk, each striding rhythmically in a solid march.

As the old hymn goes, "All good gifts around us are sent from heaven above. So thank the Lord, oh thank the Lord, for all his love." Yet how often do we attribute the source of treasures to the One who has provided them? One servant, when given a gift of talents with which to work, squandered it. Two servants took their talents, used them, and glorified their lord by increasing their talents and returning that increase to him.

American founding father Benjamin Franklin said, "Certainty? In this world nothing is certain but death and taxes."[11] We can fear death. Or we can allow our active faith in the One who has set eternity in our hearts, the God who gives the spirit of life, to diminish our dread of death. We can put our trust in the words of the Apostle Paul who, when talking about death, wrote:

11 http://www.brainyquote.com/quotes/quotes/b/benjaminfr151592.html

> "Where, O death, is your victory?
> Where, O death, is your sting?"
> The sting of death is sin, and the power of sin is the law. But thanks be to God! He gives us the victory through our Lord Jesus Christ. (1 Corinthians 15:55–57)

Life is filled with choices. As far as platitudes go, this one is trite but true, understated but understood. The Teacher, looking back on a life filled with choices, said that only one choice mattered. The end of the matter, says the Teacher, is to glorify God with our choices.

Only then will life, under the sun, be more than a meaningless chasing of the wind.

Discussion Questions

Focus

1. What do you want to hear at your funeral? Try writing out your own eulogy.

Zoom In

2. Which of the three themes of Ecclesiastes—"Meaningless, Meaningless," "Chasing the Wind," or "Under the Son"—resonates with you the deepest?

3. Which of these—wisdom, wishes, work, desires, deeds, toil, treasure, and termination—are you using to serve God? To serve yourself?

Develop

4. How can we learn to trust God—even in the face of death?